A Day in the Life c

Nurse

Carol Watson

FRANKLIN WATTS
LONDON•SYDNEY

Michelle is a nurse in the
children's ward of a large
hospital. She starts her day
by changing into her uniform.

First Michelle asks for the latest
information on the patients.
Then she tells the details to a
member of her team on the ward.

"We have a new patient coming in for a tonsil operation," says Michelle. She and her team make up the beds for all the new patients.

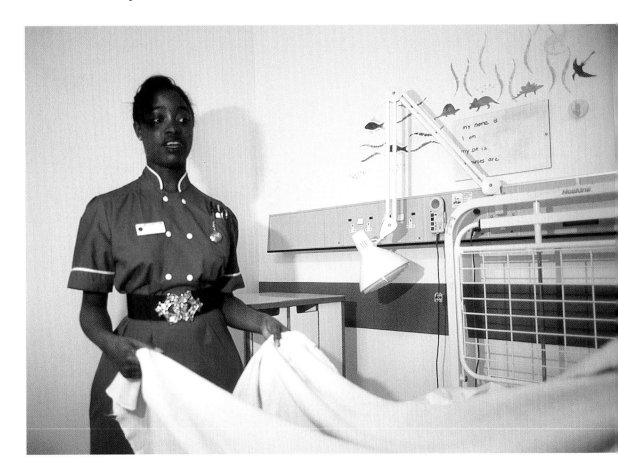

Later, Michelle welcomes the new patient as she arrives with her mum.
"Hello, Gemma," she says.
"We're all ready for you."

Michelle shows the patient and her mum onto the ward. She writes Gemma's name and age above the bed.

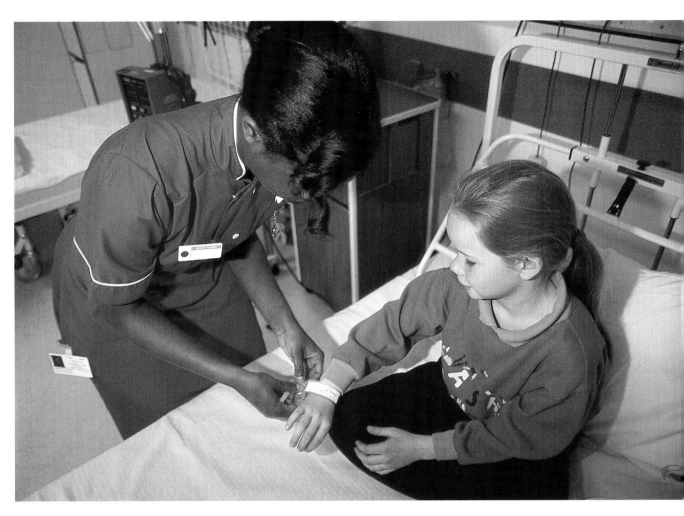

"We put your name on your
wrist, too," says Michelle.
She fastens a plastic name
tab around Gemma's arm.

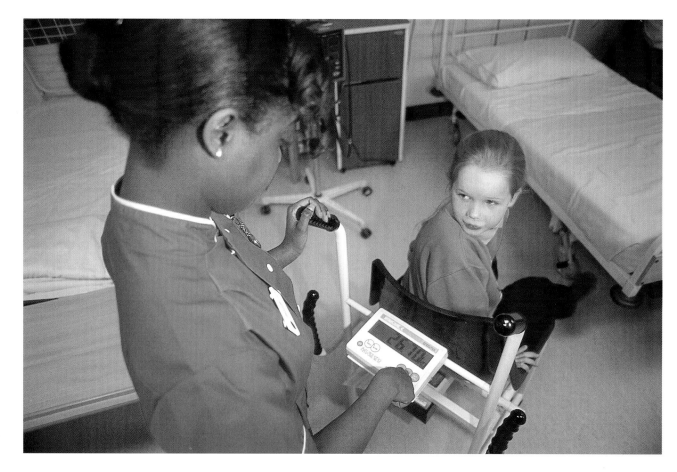

Next Michelle weighs Gemma
in a special chair. She also takes
her blood pressure which is
measured on a machine.

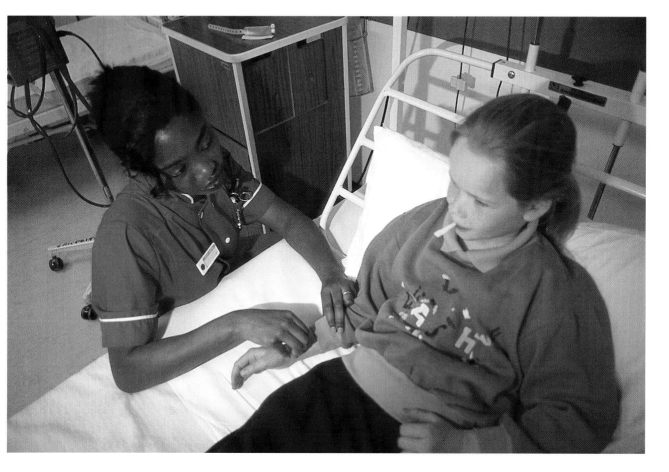

Michelle puts a thermometer
strip into Gemma's mouth and
takes her pulse. "Your temperature
is normal," she tells Gemma.

Michelle writes down information about Gemma. "Is there anything you can't eat?" she asks her. She tells Gemma about the operation and shows her what she will wear.

After that Michelle takes Gemma
to the play area, where she
meets other patients.
"There are all sorts of interesting
books to read," she tells Gemma.

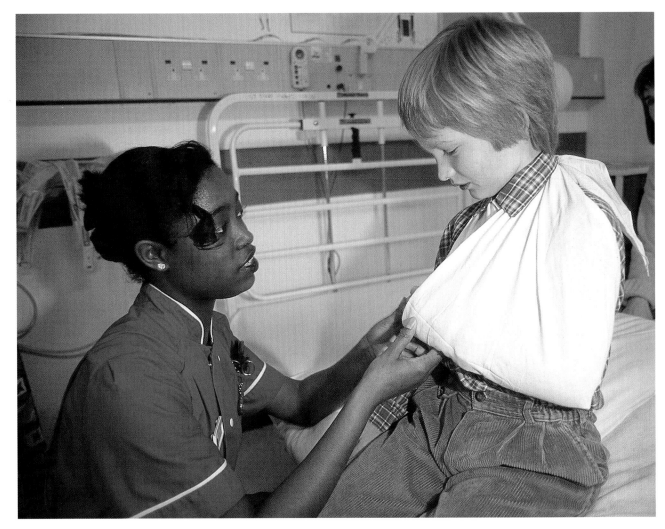

Once Gemma is settled in, Michelle
checks on her other patients.
"How is your arm feeling today?"
she asks Rupert.

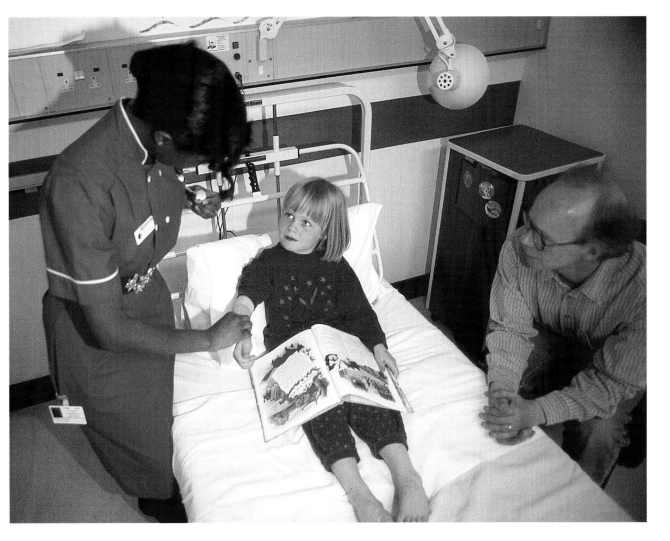

Bella is recovering from an appendix operation. Michelle takes her pulse and temperature to see if they are back to normal.

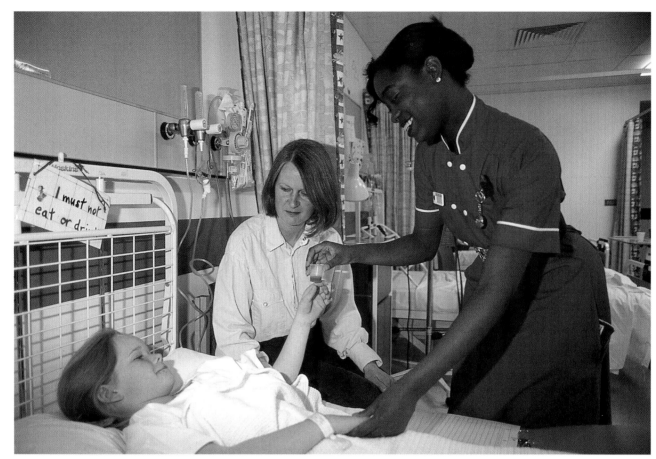

Soon it's time to prepare
Gemma for her operation.
"This medicine will make
you feel sleepy," says Michelle.

Once Gemma is asleep she is wheeled out of the ward and a porter takes her to the operating theatre.

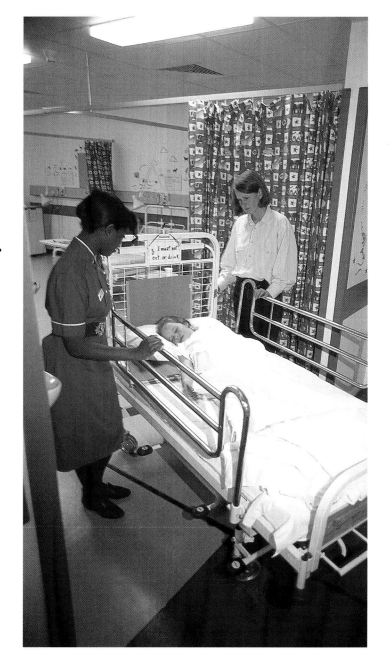

15

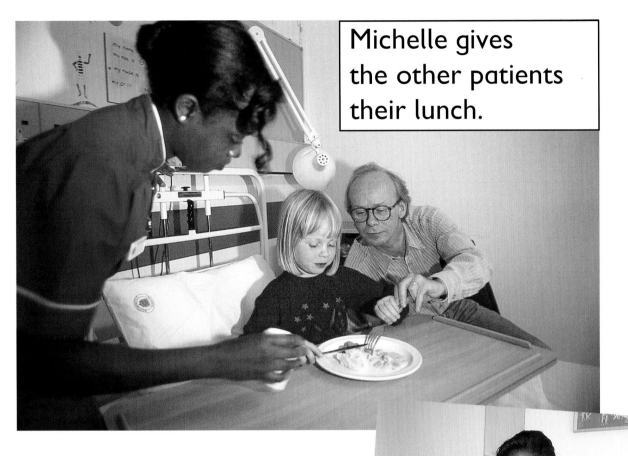

Michelle gives the other patients their lunch.

Then she goes to the nurse's room to have her lunch, too.

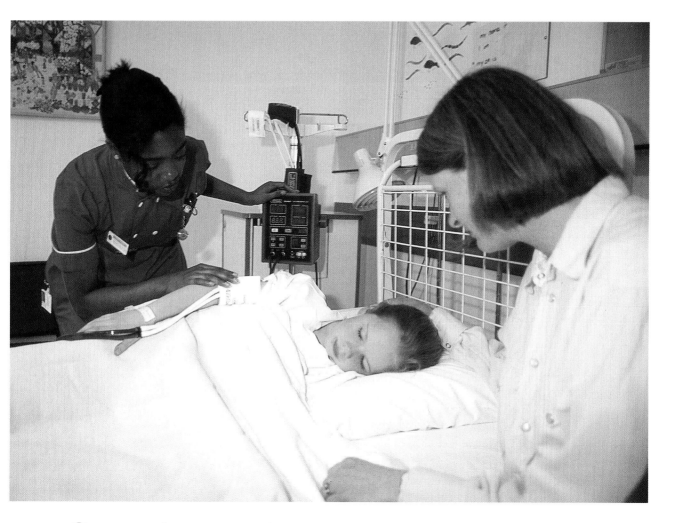

Gemma's operation is over.
Michelle takes her mum to
see her in the recovery room.
Back in the ward, she checks
Gemma's blood pressure and pulse.

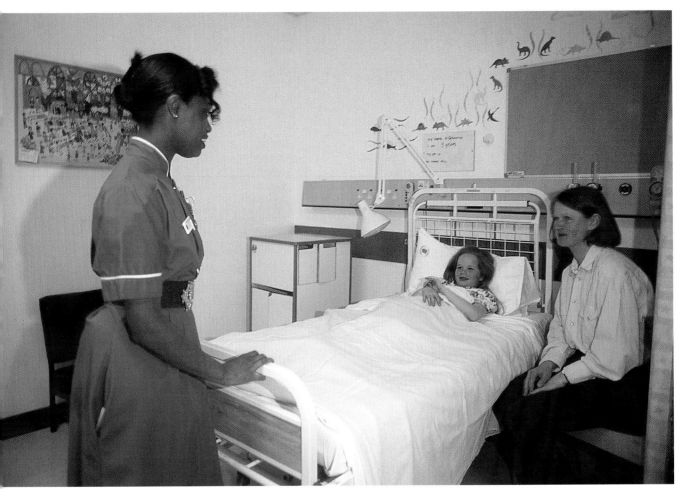

"Your operation went well,"
Michelle tells Gemma.
"I'm going off duty now.
I'll see you tomorrow."

Michelle changes
out of her
uniform and
sets off
for home.

Simple First Aid

If you want to help yourself and others here are some useful hints:-

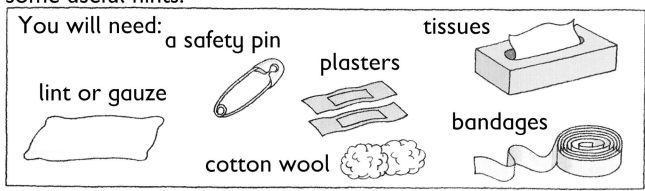

You will need:

lint or gauze

a safety pin

plasters

cotton wool

tissues

bandages

Cuts and grazes

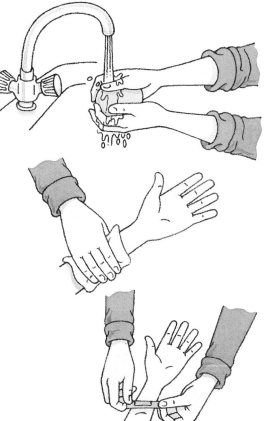

1. Before you clean a wound always wash your hands.

2. Gently clean the cut with cotton wool and warm water. Dry it with a clean towel or tissue.

3. Put a piece of plaster over the wound to keep it germ-free.

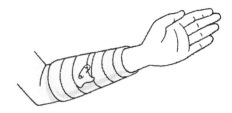

4. If it is a large cut, put a piece of lint or gauze over it and wrap a bandage round it to keep it in place. Fasten with a safety pin.

Burns or scalds

1. If you burn or scald yourself always put that part of your body in cold water for ten minutes. This will take the heat out of the skin.

2. Dry it gently with a clean towel or tissue, and then cover it with something clean and dry. A tissue will do. Tie it on with some bandage.

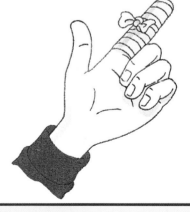

Always tell an adult if you are hurt.

How you can help nurses if you go into hospital

1. Make sure you tell the nurse if there is anything you shouldn't eat or drink.

2. Don't ever eat or drink anything if the nurse tells you not to.

3. Tell your nurse if you are feeling sick, or hurting.

4. Don't touch any of the machines on the ward.

5. Never leave the ward without your parent or a nurse.

6. Take your favourite cuddly toy or book to read.

Facts about nurses

To become a nurse you need to go to a college or university and take a course that lasts three years. When this is completed successfully a nurse is qualified at the first level.

After working for some time at the first level, a registered nurse can move up to a different level. The nurse in this book is a staff nurse. She has worked for over three years since she qualified.

The person in charge of the ward is called the sister. Below her there are senior staff nurses, staff nurses and student nurses. Nurses wear different coloured uniforms and belts to show which level they are at. These vary in different hospitals.

Michelle trained especially to look after sick children. Other nurses train to look after adults, mentally handicapped patients or people who are mentally ill.

Index

© 1996 Franklin Watts

This edition 2001

Franklin Watts
96 Leonard Street
London EC2A 4XD

Franklin Watts Australia
56 O'Riordan Street
Alexandria, Sydney, NSW 2015

ISBN 0 7496 4103 7

Dewey Decimal Classification
Number 610.73

10 9 8 7 6 5 4 3 2

Editor: Sarah Ridley
Design: Kirstie Billingham
Photography: Chris Honeywell
Illustration: MIchael Evans

With thanks to the Osborne
family, Christopher, Caroline and
Rupert Compston, the staff at
Chelsea and Westminster
Hospital, Michelle Ellis and
Mr Jeremy Booth.

A CIP catalogue record for this book
is available from the British Library.

Printed in Malaysia